GARDEN
IDEAS

KU-617-050

GARDEN IDEAS

Elizabeth Keevill

hamlyn

contents

From the royal gardens of ancient Mesopotamia and the Hanging Gardens of Babylon to the modern urban roof terrace, we can trace the development of the garden as a place for both creative expression and

INTRODUCTION

practical activities. Since the birth of civilisation we have created outdoor spaces for reasons that reflect our need for relaxation, exercise and quiet contemplation and recognise the beneficial effects of spending our leisure time out of doors.

THE MEDIEVAL ENCLOSED GARDEN, the botanical gardens of the Renaissance, the classic formal gardens of Versailles and the Arcadian beauty of Capability Brown's landscaped gardens, all form part of a rich tradition. This is the heritage of the modern gardener, no matter how limited their experience or humble their plot of land.

We live in times of rapid development and changing attitudes. If we think about the kind of garden we knew as children – and certainly the gardens our parents sat and played in – we picture the well-tended lawn and the herbaceous border with its mixture of annuals, perennials and shrubs. If there was an all-weather area it was a rather bare patio, home to the dog kennel, dustbin or washing line. Gardens were principally places for gardening and for the passive enjoyment of the fruits of that gardening. From September to May, they were places seldom visited for any other reason than the undertaking of mundane gardening tasks.

Unless you happened to be an enthusiastic gardener with a lot of leisure time, the small urban garden tended to be a rather sterile place. It neither reflected the rich tradition of the English garden nor did it provide a particularly pleasant place to be on any but the warmest day.

Today, thankfully, things are very different. Foreign travel has made us aware to all kinds of new possibilities when it comes to the outdoor areas of our home. The Mediterranean lifestyle places a much greater emphasis on open-air living. Most eating is al fresco and no Mediterranean day is complete without a family stroll in the balmy warmth of the evening. The joy of a meal under the stars or in the shade of a fragrant pergola, and the

pleasure of the afternoon nap under a shady tree, are essential ingredients of the Mediterranean lifestyle.

In sunnier climes, people regard outdoor areas as the natural extension of even the humblest home. Tables and chairs are dragged outside for meals. Fresh herbs are cultivated to add essential flavouring to food. Flowers are grown simply for their beauty. Trees and climbing plants provide natural and very necessary shade in the heat of the day. Even if there is only space for a seat and a few pot plants outside the front of the house, perhaps under a window sill brimming with geraniums, this is enough to enjoy the sensual pleasures of the garden.

This idea of the outside room is rapidly gaining popularity in Britain. In our increasingly hectic lives we really appreciate a place that not only allows us scope for creative expression, but that provides a place in the open air where we can relax, socialise and eat. Rather than thinking of gardens as essentially separate from the house, we can now consider the two together as one homogenous living area. With thought, we can create an environment where the outdoor areas become natural extensions of indoors.

Over the past twenty years, we have become ever more interested in the way we furnish and decorate our homes.

The democratisation of interior design has allowed us to express our individuality and enabled us to tailor our homes to our individual requirements. The growing number and popularity of home interest magazines and television programmes about home improvements reflect our much more flexible attitude to home design and the creative explosion of ideas in this area.

This increasing awareness of interior design can be extended to embrace the way we look at our garden, roof terrace or balcony. Just as interior design is now an idea familiar to all, we need to think about exterior design if we are to be successful in producing outside rooms.

Making decorative items for the home, experimenting with colour, and renovating old furniture are popular trends in DIY. Mosaic, broken colour effects and painting murals: all of these creative and rewarding activities can be applied to outside rooms as well, producing exciting, eye-catching results.

More than ever, space is at a premium. We have to make sure that each part of our home makes efficient use of available space. This principle is equally important when we are thinking out the layout of our outside room. Space is used more efficiently when the amount of time for which it can be used is maximised. The old-fashioned suburban garden, only really used for a couple of months

in the summer and seldom entered after night fall, will not satisfy the needs of our modern lifestyle.

In our outside room we need areas that are all-weather, which we can use after rain when conditions underfoot are damp. In the garden, just as in any other room we need some form of lighting – both to enjoy the romantic barbecue and bottle of well-chilled wine under the stars on a balmy evening, and to appreciate the beauty of our garden from the cosiness of indoors on bleak winter nights.

Unless we are genuinely interested in gardening for its own sake, the growing and tending of plants and shrubs are simply means to an end, although a very satisfying activity. Few of us want to spend all our leisure time decorating our home. What we really want to do is spend time relaxing in it after the decorating is finished. Although plants are an essential and extremely beautiful part of any garden, we need to find ways to ensure that when we are in the garden we are not spending all our time weeding, pruning and tidying.

This book will help you to start thinking about your outdoor spaces as outdoor rooms, as real extensions of your living areas. It will inspire you with simple ideas to start creating beautiful, practical open-air spaces that you will enjoy throughout the year.

It will show you how other people have approached exterior design and produced stunning results, sometimes in the smallest, most unlikely places. It will introduce you to unusual, low maintenance ways to grow and display your plants in even the most confined space. Throughout the book there are simple, creative projects for you to try too, that will help make your garden not only a more interesting place to relax in, but also an expression of your personality.

If all you have is a balcony – or even just a window sill – do not despair. With a little imagination you can extend your living area outdoors and start to really enjoy the pleasures of growing plants and the healthy benefits of relaxing in the open air.

Boundaries form a link and a barrier between us and the outside world. Fences and hedges, walls or neighbouring buildings, they form the outline of our outdoor space and mark the area that we can plan and influence unhindered. Gardens can be magical places and that magic starts with the way we deal with their boundaries.

WALL TO WALL

Think about doorways and windows and consider the view both from inside and out. Create a memorable impression for your visitors by paying attention to gates, paths and entrances.

10

climbing and creeping plants

URBAN GARDENS ARE USUALLY SURROUNDED by neighbours' walls or fences. Creepers and climbing plants provide colourful cover for unattractive surfaces. Climbing plants can look stunning on the exteriors of houses, giving distinction to even the blandest of architecture. Even where there is no soil, many varieties are happy growing in pots or troughs and some thrive with their roots in an enclosed environment. Where planting space is limited, creepers and climbers are a particularly good choice, giving height, colour and texture from a small area of ground.

PLANTING TRICKS

Some varieties of climbing plants, notably Virginia Creeper and most types of ivy, need no supporting structure. Their adhesive tendrils cling to any tiny crevices. Sweet peas and morning glory will only require a lightweight structure, while wisteria and laburnum will need something more substantial. If possible, erect any supports before planting and anticipate the mature size of your plants.

GROUND RULES

There are many different ways to support climbing plants, depending on the variety you choose. Trellis, tensionable wires, netting and even string can be used but whatever you choose, make sure it is well secured before planting. Once your plants are growing it is extremely difficult to repair or extend the support without causing damage. Keep climbing plants, other than creepers, 3–5 cm away from any wall by mounting these supports on battens. This will help prevent damp and mildew by allowing air to circulate.

Inspirations

Informally trained up a wall, plants can provide a link between the garden and its boundaries. Combine climbing plants with containers of low level flowering plants on the ground to give additional interest. You can train climbers across corners as they mature to provide shade and add another dimension to your garden.

PLANTING TRICKS

If you need to cover an eyesore, choose fast growing plants like passion flower or ivy. When planting in beds, site the roots away from the base of the wall as rain water runoff can cause waterlogging. Tie new shoots loosely to your support to leave room for growth.

Inspirations

Even attractive walls and doorways can benefit from a framework of climbing plants. Ivies are happiest in shady or partly shaded areas, whereas honeysuckle and roses thrive in sunny spots.

THE PLANTS

Clematis
Hedera (Ivy)
Humulus (Hop)
Lathyrus (Sweet Pea)
Lonicera (Honeysuckle)
Parthenocissus (Virginia Creeper)
Rosa (Climbing Rose)
Wisteria

special effects

AN ENCLOSED AREA can be beautifully transformed by changing the backdrop against which the plants are grown. Choosing a bright colour can make an enormous difference to your garden during the winter months when there is less colour in the plants, pots and containers. The pictures below show how the application of a coat of exterior paint in a bold shade on a dark wall can create a tropical mood, a Tuscan patio or simply offer a glorious sunny outlook on the bleakest of November days. Hardware stores now offer a great choice of paint in a variety of different colours, so you can literally change the colour of your garden wall according to your mood.

YOU WILL NEED
a wire brush
a paintbrush
exterior filler
sandpaper
exterior emulsion paint in a colour of your choice

TUSCAN MOOD
Before applying the paint, make sure that the surface is clean, dry and dust free. Remove any loose paint or stucco with a wire brush. Fill any cracks in the wall with filler. When this is dry sand down.

TROPICAL SUNSET
Apply two coats of exterior emulsion in the colour of your choice. One litre of paint will cover approximately 15 sq m (17 sq yd) of previously decorated surface.

14

changing views

EVEN THE MOST INTIMATE COURTYARD GARDEN can provide an abundance of opportunities for imaginative planting. Where floor space is limited, walls and window sills are ideal areas for creative gardening. As well as increasing your growing area, vertical planting can soften the effect of high walls and can turn an eyesore into an attractive feature. Any vertical planting must be very securely attached and fixings should be regularly inspected and replaced. The most lightweight basket can double or treble in weight when filled with crocks, damp soil and plants.

PLANTING TRICKS

Be generous when planting wall baskets. Your aim should be to create a sense of abundance. Remember that you will be looking upwards at most of your plants so favour varieties that tend to trail such as trailing fuchsias, peonies and pelargoniums. If you are using wire baskets, punch holes in the liners and insert further plants around the sides and bottom. For really hardworking basket displays, mix a selection of low-growing and trailing plants.

Inspirations

Think carefully about the general effect your plantings will have. Aim to create bold blocks of colour. All colours look particularly effective against lush foliage and the combination of flowers, foliage and brickwork can turn a dull wall into a truly memorable display. You can also hang container displays from trees or free standing trellis.

GARDEN WISDOM

The warmth retained by walls in sunny spots can quickly dry out planters so they need regular tending. Moss lining, a layer of absorbent ceramic pebbles and good quality potting medium will all help to retain moisture but all containers, wherever they are sited, will need regular watering and misting. Pump sprays make watering high-up plants easier.

Inspirations

Painting your walls white up to the top of your display creates a Mediterranean effect. It also provides a contrasting backdrop for your plants, drawing the eye away from duller brickwork above. Containers at ground level lend weight to the arrangement.

THE PLANTS

Chrysanthemum
   (Marguerite Daisy)
Crocus
Cyclamen
Muscari (Grape Hyacinth)
Narcissus
Polypodium (Fern)
Primula
Saxifraga (Saxifrage)

pots and plants

URNS AND PLANTERS HAVE ALWAYS BEEN an essential element of the traditional garden. Containers are again fashionable, especially in town gardens where space may be very limited. It is now possible to find a variety of containers, planters and pots in garden centres in stunning designs.

Containers come in all shapes and sizes and it is perfectly feasible to grow large imposing plants and even small trees in pots. Once planted, large containers can prove extremely heavy so you should regard them as semi-permanent features.

GROUND RULES

Containers must be stable and ideally you should position them on a solid surface rather than on a lawn or on soil. They must also be weighty enough for the size of plant: a top-heavy shrub, for example, could otherwise be blown over in strong winds. Containers must also be frost-proof as however beautiful, pots are no use if they crack apart in the middle of winter.

THE PLANTS

Argyranthemum
Brassica (Ornamental Cabbage)
Erica (Heathers)
Euonymus
Hyacinthus (Hyacinth)
Narcissus
Senecio
Solanum

Inspirations
Informal arrangements can often work surprisingly well, especially if you use unusual containers. Galvanised watering cans that have sprung a leak or buckets that have outlived their use make wonderful planters. Ornamental cabbages bring a colourful touch of humour and, being compact, don't obscure their containers.

GARDEN WISDOM

If you use discarded items as planters you need to follow some simple rules. Make sure any container allows sufficient drainage. Drill holes in the base and put a layer of stones or broken pots in the bottom to prevent the soil from becoming waterlogged. Line wooden containers with plastic to help protect them from rotting.

Inspirations

Plants in pots can be quickly assembled into a stunning display, especially when grouped around a strong central feature. Some plant containers, like this classic urn, are pieces of sculpture in their own right. Take care to match containers to their surroundings both in style and scale.

IDEAS

It can be extremely satisfying to recycle old things and give them a new lease of life in your garden. Wheelbarrows brimming over with flowers, old chimney stacks of different heights, Belfast sinks and discarded galvanised containers can look wonderful when sympathetically grouped. However, beware of overdoing things or you may end up with just an ill-assorted jumble.

GROUND RULES

When looking for containers make sure they are genuinely frost-proof and have adequate means of drainage. Avoid containers that curve in excessively towards the top as these make transplanting difficult and, even if frost-proof, can crack when frozen soil inside expands. Modern reproductions of classical urns can often make a satisfactory substitute for the genuine article.

mosaic tile table top

BRIGHTEN UP YOUR GARDEN with this colourful, easy to make mosaic table top. You can apply the mosaic pieces directly on to an existing table or on to a new top made from MDF or plywood. To make a new top you will need to make it 10 cm larger all round than the table you wish to cover. You will also need to secure it by attaching four 5 cm battens to the underside, each parallel to and 5 cm from the edges. As these are not load-bearing they can be glued in place with wood adhesive. If the existing table is circular a new square top will measure 10 cm larger on each side than the diameter of the circular table.

STEP 1

Apply 2 coats of diluted PVA adhesive to the surface paying attention to the edges. Wrap each tile in an old towel and break them with a hammer. Set aside the broken pieces in a box.

YOU WILL NEED

table top or MDF or plywood
    approx. 12mm thick, cut to
    size
4 x 5 cm battens (top only)
PVA glue, diluted
tiles, (approx. 25). 10 x 10cm
tile adhesive
spreader
tile grout
goggles
gloves
old tea towel
hammer
soft cloth
beading
panel pins

STEP 2

With the spreader, spread the tile adhesive over part of the top to a depth of 2–3mm, arrange the broken tiles as you go leaving a small gap between each. Make sure the glazed edges face forward to give a smooth edge. Continue until the table is covered, filling any gaps with small pieces – leave to dry.

STEP 3

Rinse the spreader and use it to fill the gaps between the tiles with grout, either white or coloured. Clean off any excess and leave to dry overnight. Fill in any remaining gaps with grout. When dry, polish with a dry cloth. If your mosaic is on an existing table, attach beading to the same depth as the raised surface of the mosaic using panel pins. If MDF or plywood is used paint the edge with emulsion in a colour of your choice.

gateways and doorways

GATEWAYS AND DOORS ARE THE FIRST IMPRESSIONS a visitor has of your home and the first thing you encounter on your return after a busy day. Entrances set the tone for what lies beyond and are the ideal places to introduce themes that you want to develop more fully in the rest of your house and garden. Roses around the door are the very essence of the cottage garden, while the town front door, flanked by standard bay trees in their wooden Versailles tubs, suggests the formal symmetry of the Georgian era. Soften front steps by adding a cascade of potted plants down each side.

PLANTING TRICKS

Containers around the door bring a feeling of colour and warmth to your home even before you or your guests enter. Choose containers and plants that complement the building materials of the house and the style of your doorways. Be generous when planting containers for entrances as this will reinforce the welcoming message. Take into account the aspect when choosing plants. Doorways can be sunny or spend most of the day in shade so you need plants that will cope with these conditions.

Inspirations

Decorative gates can give an enticing preview of your garden. Little-used entrances can be piled up at the bottom with containers to make a perfect frame for the view inside. Gates left ajar arouse curiosity and invite further investigation. The gate itself becomes part of the display, making an attractive contrast with the vista beyond.

THE PLANTS

Azalea
Chrysanthemum
Clematis
Eschscholzia
Myosotis
Papaver (Poppies)
Perlargoniums
Solidago

Inspirations

It would be hard to imagine a cottage door without its hanging baskets. Side entrances and garage doors also benefit from generous plantings, while window boxes will add a further welcoming touch for visitors to your home. For a well thought-out look, put the same varieties in all the containers.

PLANTING TRICKS

Building a structure that suggests a gateway can add a stunning focal point to a plain and simple garden. Trellis part way down a long lawn can break up a dreary view and add mystery to what lies beyond. A simple arch, planted with clematis or climbing roses, can form a transitional area that you can further enhance with a bold display of containers at its base. A bird bath or statue will give added interest to the arrangement.

making an entrance

WHY NOT ADD A TOUCH OF DRAMA to your garden with this effective false gate or door? You can either paint a landscape behind a false gate creating the illusion of a distant vista outside the garden wall or secure a solid false door to your garden wall to hint at the possibility of a secret garden beyond. Both of these ideas are fun to create and add a touch of drama in a plain garden wall. We have chosen a simple landscape scene, however you can be as creative as you like. The doorway will look more realistic if you trail some plants around the harsh edges.

YOU WILL NEED

1 large piece of plywood or MDF cut to the size of a gateway
1 gate (reclaimed)
1 pot of white emulsion
1 pot of green poster paint
1 pot of blue poster paint (diluted 2 parts to 1)
1 paint brush
1 sponge
pebbles or gravel

STEP 1

Paint the top two thirds of one side of your MDF with white emulsion, this will be the base coat of the sky. When this is dry, paint over the emulsion with the watered down blue paint, in different directions brush to create a dappled sky effect. Leave to dry.

STEP 2

Sponge the bottom third of the MDF with the green paint to give the impression of grass on a distant hillside. Allow to dry.

STEP 3

Lean the MDF against a stretch of garden wall, place the gate in front at the bottom. Complete the look by scattering gravel or pebbles at the base, in front of the gate.

NO ENTRY?

This beautiful al fresco setting is complemented by the illusion of a country scene beyond a doorway. It gives the garden a whole new perspective creating the illusion of greater depth and space. Arrange pots and plants around the base and tease tendrils of climbing plants around the sides of the gate to give a sense of permanence.

shelf life

THE SECRET OF SUCCESSFUL GARDENING where space is limited is to make maximum use of what little space you do have. This type of gardening requires imagination, careful planning and discipline but you can achieve spectacular results. Imaginative use of shelving is one of the quickest ways to extend the planting area of your garden. Simple shelves fixed to a wall with brackets, greenhouse staging and rustic trellis work can all provide attractive new areas to grow and display plants. Shelves also change perspectives and provide new dimensions for your overall design.

GROUND RULES

Variations in height are important. When growing areas are raised, the eye naturally travels upwards, making high walls less oppressive. Shelves can be made of wood (marine ply is suitable), moisture resistant MDF (medium density fibreboard) or galvanised metal. Fix shelves to garden walls rather than to the house as accumulated water could cause damp.

GARDEN WISDOM

Originally designed to make working on plants at different levels easier, greenhouse staging is also ideal for displaying container plants in an effective and space-efficient way. Placed against a wall, metal staging provides low maintenance and instant terracing exactly where you want it. Arranging two sets of staging back-to-back makes a stunning dividing wall or central display.

Inspirations

Low-tech solutions can provide a refreshing change from the uniform patterns of manufactured trellis work. A free-standing rustic framework can be attached to a wall just as easily. As well as providing a climbing frame for sweet peas, it makes an unusual structure from which to suspend the growing pots.

PLANTING TRICKS

Greenhouse staging can be planted with a great variety of different species. There is something almost theatrical about arranging plants outdoors in this way. Don't be afraid to contrast colours and heights, taking advantage of the terracing effect to give all the plants maximum light. Rearrange your displays periodically and be ruthless about removing plants that are past their best.

THE PLANTS

Chrysanthemum
Dahlia
Helichrysum
Hydrangea
Lathyrus (Sweet Pea)
Lilium (Lilies)
Myosotis
Perlargonium

Inspirations

MDF, which you can buy in a moisture-resistant form, is a wonderfully versatile material for DIY and is easy to work with. Here two rows of red zonal pelargoniums have been slotted into holes cut in painted MDF shelving to make a stunning display of uniform blooms.

GROUND RULES

With shelves in particular, it is important to aim for a bold clean effect. Shelves in your home or garden look dreadful heaped up with a jumble of items. Paint shelving with exterior quality paint to protect it from moisture. Be bold with your choice of colour and make a feature of the shelves by choosing a colour to contrast with the plants.

behind the screen

ALTHOUGH ASSOCIATED WITH BLOOMS and tended displays, gardens often end up also playing host to such unattractive necessities as dustbins, heating oil tanks, compost heaps and washing lines. However important these things may be, you do not want to be constantly aware of them. A solution to this problem is to screen off such areas. However, human nature makes us want to know what is behind any sort of barrier, so screening should be tackled with subtlety. When screens are successful, they can add important extra dimensions and perspectives to your garden. Another solution is to divert the eye away from eyesores by creating a more interesting focal point nearby.

GROUND RULES

A quick way to disguise eyesores is with free-standing trellis or fencing, which provides an instant screen for training climbing plants. Trellis comes in a variety of designs and in varying qualities. Buying cheap trellis or fencing can prove a false economy if it collapses with a beautiful plant growing up it. Get the best you can afford and make sure it has been properly weatherproofed. Any nails and fixings should be galvanised.

PLANTING TRICKS

Planting up both sides of a fence or free-standing trellis screen will produce a lush, dense effect. Offset the roots on either side of the screen to avoid plants fighting for nutrients from the same patch of soil. Choose plants that bloom at different times of the year for longer flowering interest. Make sure at least some of your screen is planted with evergreens, such as ivy, or the screening effect will be lost in winter.

Inspirations

One way to disguise unsightly objects is to draw the eye away from them. A colourful display of blooms distracts attention from the dustbins housed below and adds interest to the view from the house. The addition of cushions transforms the ingenious clothes-drying chest above into a comfortable bench.

GARDEN WISDOM

The most important aspect to consider when planning a screen is the view from your house. Overdo screening and you will just draw attention to the thing you are trying to disguise. The best solution can be to draw attention from the area by creating a focal point such as a bold display of flowers nearby and only partially disguise the offending item.

Screening isn't just for things you can see. Solid hedges can also help to reduce extraneous traffic noise.

THE PLANTS

Buxus (Box)
Chamaecyparis
Fagus (Beech)
Impatiens (Busy Lizzie)
Leylandii
Taxus (Yew)
Thuja (Western Red Cedar)
Viburnum

Patios, balconies, roof terraces and conservatories are all extensions of your home that allow you to enjoy the pleasures of gardening and eating – or simply relaxing – in the open air. No matter how small your outdoor space,

A ROOM OUTSIDE

there are lots of things you can do to make it special. Even the smallest balcony can provide room for al fresco living and luxuriant plant displays that can be enjoyed by you, your guests and even passers-by.

patios and conservatories

GARDENS CAN BE DIVIDED into hard and soft-surfaced areas. Soft areas – principally lawns – are fine in summer, when they can be enjoyed at their best. However in spring, autumn and winter a wet or muddy lawn has limited use. Hard areas – patios, conservatories and terraces – are practical places which you can use and enjoy throughout the year. A hardworking garden has to have all-weather areas, plan your garden as a whole and make sure that the hard and soft areas complement each other rather than being separate entities.

GROUND RULES

A well-integrated patio gives a clean, sheltered and easily maintained area for sitting, eating and even preparing and cooking food. Always consider the practical uses of hard outdoor areas when planning them. Patios can also be excellent places for young children to play outside when the lawn is wet. They are also good places to site a retractable clothes line so you don't have to squelch across the grass to collect your washing.

Inspirations

Plants are shown off to great effect on decking. These hyacinths look fabulous against the dark background and their curvaceous semi-glazed planters contrast with – and soften – the uniform timber planking. The white steamer chair makes a further contrast with the decking while echoing the overall colonial style.

PLANTING TRICKS

Low walls, often used to define patio areas, look stunning if constructed with room for planting in the top. Filled with flowering and trailing plants, they help to blur the transition from soft to hard areas. Use containers and troughs instead of walls for a more informal boundary.

GARDEN WISDOM

Conservatories create a bridge between the garden and the house and are ideal for use in inclement weather or as a shady retreat. Blinds are a wise investment for protecting both plants and humans from the effects of the midday sun and for heat conservation in the winter.

THE PLANTS

Hibiscus

Jasminum (Jasmine)

Lavatera

Lilium (Lilies)

Muscari (Grape Hyacinth)

Perlargonium

Petunia

Viola (Pansies)

PLANTING TRICKS

Dark shady areas, often found to the side of houses and often neglected, can make ideal places for secluded patios. Shade-loving ferns grown in containers, dark green iron furniture and brick paving can combine to make a wonderful spot to escape from the heat of the day and enjoy the garden beyond. The courtyard effect is very pleasing. A simple bowl of fruit on the table introduces a splash of colour.

room to grow

IN ANY GARDEN, EFFECTIVE USE OF SPACE is important, but when ground area is limited, every square centimetre counts. There is no outdoor space too small to grow something attractive. It is simply a matter of choosing the right plants. While the herbaceous border is the traditional place to show off shrubs and flowers, well thought-out container displays not only look beautiful, they also beautify their surroundings. Small scale gardening brings you much closer to your plants and being able to sit among them is a very different experience from simply standing and looking at them.

GARDEN WISDOM

The marvellous thing about containers is their versatility. Plants can be moved around to change the display and to discover where they are happiest growing. Don't be afraid to replace plants when they are past their best. Be sure to check their mature size when you choose varieties for container planting and favour those with long flowering periods. Everything has to work hard in restricted spaces so plants that look good even when not in bloom are wise choices.

Inspirations

Making use of every available space is the key to the successful small garden. Hang shade-loving plants under shelves arranged with plants that prefer a sunny aspect. Combine flowering plants with foliage varieties for year-round displays. Variegated plants can make an interesting feature in their own right.

THE PLANTS

Aster
Aubrieta
Begonia
Euphorbia
Orchidaceae (Orchids)
Poinsettia
Polyanthus
Primula

PLANTING TRICKS

Spring is an exciting time in the container garden. Early-flowering bulbs, such as narcissus and hyacinth, planted in autumn, are a delightful harbinger of the better weather to come. Many spring-flowering shrubs – azaleas, rhododendrons and camellias for example – also do well in containers.

GROUND RULES

Selecting the right
containers is just as
important as choosing the
plants to go in them. On
balconies and roof terraces
the priority with pots is
lightness. For other parts of
the garden you can choose
from a huge array of styles
and materials.

Inspirations

*A concentrated mass of
flowering plants and
shrubs can transform a
simple window ledge into
a magnificent feature.
Keeping plants in individual
containers makes regular
maintenance straightforward
and allows you to rearrange
your display periodically and
replace plants that have
finished flowering. An old
trug makes an attractive
planter.*

painted pots

AN ECONOMICAL AND EASY WAY to brighten up your garden is to decorate terra-cotta flower pots with bold colours and designs. This project is so simple and fun that all the family can be involved including children, although they should be supervised. You can experiment with different designs and colours, these decorated pots will also make great presents for friends and family and can be personalised accordingly. All you need is a little imagination to achieve fantastic results. You can even afford to bring the garden indoors, jazz up herbs for your window sill or a Yucca for your living room.

YOU WILL NEED

2 large flower pots in terra-cotta
6 medium terracotta pots
white spirit and a rag
250 ml tester pots, emulsion, matt yellow, orange and pink, dark green, bright green and blue
masking tape 2.5 cm wide
scissors
undercoat, white
paint brushes, as many as you like

STEP 1
For this project it is best to buy new flower pots – make sure the pots are totally dry and clean before paint is applied. Apply one coat of white undercoat with a brush, when this is dry apply the colour of your choice.

STEP 2
When the paint is dry cut shapes or stripes out of masking tape and stick to the pot in a design of your choice. Paint over the masking tape covering the entire pot in a contrasting colour and leave to dry.

STEP 3
When the second coat of paint is dry carefully remove the masking tape. You can continue the process to build up as many colours as you like. Finally seal with acrylic matt varnish. This will prevent the paint from running and ensure that the pot continues to look good.

eating out

ONE OF THE GREAT PLEASURES IN LIFE is tending and enjoying your garden, another is eating. Combining the two is always a wonderful experience but climate does not always allow for true 'al fresco' eating, which you can safely plan in advance. However it is easy to transform rooms that allow you to live 'outside' inside – conservatories, enclosed balconies and even greenhouses – into areas where you can dine under the stars even when there's snow on the ground. Details are important so pay particular attention to lighting and place settings.

INSIDE OUTSIDE

Conservatories were originally upmarket greenhouses attached to the house where plants could be enjoyed throughout the year. Increasingly, conservatories are an extension of the living area, many are still used primarily as greenhouses. They make delightful places to take lunch or afternoon tea, with the essence of entertaining being to enjoy a view of the garden without having to worry about the weather.

Inspirations

Not all conservatories will be modern, double-glazed heated constructions. Enhance older conservatories with simple pieces of period furniture, trugs and tools that suggest a bygone age. Keeping the glass sparkling will greatly affect the quality of light in any conservatory both during the day and at night.

GARDEN WISDOM

Wooden, rattan or wrought iron furniture can look particularly effective for conservatory dining. Make sure whatever you choose complements the style of your conservatory and the general feel of the rest of your house. Remember bright sunlight is likely to fade and eventually rot furnishing fabrics.

GROUND RULES

To make the most use of your conservatory throughout the year, heating is an important consideration. Underfloor heating can usually run from an existing boiler and is both efficient and unobtrusive. In summer, custom-made roof blinds will help keep your conservatory cool.

Inspirations

Garden rooms can provide the perfect surroundings for an informal dinner party. White furniture and a crisp white table cloth complement the window frames, while a brick floor makes a stylish and practical compromise when plants figure in large numbers. At night create an intimate atmosphere with candles or oil lamps.

THE PLANTS

Beloperone (Shrimp Plant)
Dracaena
Helianthus (Sunflower)
Hyacinthus (Hyacinth)
Hydrangea
Pelargonium
Vitis (Grape Vine)

in the shade

**AWNING ONE
YOU WILL NEED**
3 pieces of coloured muslin,
or sheets
16 bamboo poles
twine
clothes pegs

A PICNIC IS ALWAYS GREAT FUN whether it is in the comfort of your own garden or in the countryside. There is nothing better than spending your spare time relaxing with friends and family in the great outdoors. You can create your own private space anywhere by erecting a simple awning, which will offer protection from the sun's rays. Children will be able to play safely and a meal can be enjoyed out of the heat of the midday sun. Erecting an awning is not difficult and you may well have most of the materials in the garden shed and scrap fabric bag.

STEP 1
Wind the twine around the tops of 3 of the bamboo poles (see above), repeat the process with another 3 sets of the 3 bamboo poles. Push the base of the poles firmly into the ground at least 40 cm/16 inches apart. Repeat with the other 3 sets of poles positioning them to form a square or a rectangle. These are the four corners of your awning. The size of the awning can be tailored according to your needs, but do not be too ambitious or the top may become too heavy for the supports.

STEP 2
Lay the remaining four bamboo poles across the top of the awning to make a square or a rectangle, this will help hold the structure together and support the material. Bind these poles in place with more of the twine.

STEP 3
Lay the pieces of muslin across the width of the bamboo awning and secure with clothes pegs.

AWNING TWO
YOU WILL NEED
2 bamboo poles
2 planted flower pots
1 split bamboo blind
2 guy ropes

STEP 1
Measure the distance between the fittings on the blind and mark the position on the wall for the two hooks (included with the blind). Using a masonry bit drill two holes and plug with rawl plugs. Screw in the hooks and hang the blind from them.

STEP 2
Push the bamboo poles deeply into the planted flower pots. Unroll the blind to its full extent and position the flower pots at an equal distance away from the wall, making sure that the bottom of the blind reaches the top of the poles. Push the poles carefully through the slats in the blinds, secure the guy rope to the bottom of the blind, this will keep the blind resting on the poles. However two guy ropes – one at each corner attached to the blind – would be needed for use in a high wind.

balconies

BALCONIES CAN VARY from little more than a window box to a terrace large enough to hold a party on. For many urban dwellers, a balcony is the only private outdoor space to which they have access and is a space to treasure, allowing an apartment to extend into the outside world. It gives the opportunity to experiment with plants, dine under the stars and sit in the sun. Balconies can also make a splash of colour that even passers-by in the street can enjoy. There are considerations of safety that must be taken seriously and the unique growing conditions may limit your choice of plants but a well-planned balcony can be an immensely rewarding place.

TIMESAVER

For year-round colour, balcony displays may require changing two or three times. Rather than replace the soil, leave the plants in their pots and bury them in the troughs or planters. Simply lift out the old plants at the end of their season.

PLANTING TRICKS

Plants in containers can be heavy so weight is a major consideration with balconies. As a balcony tends to be a cantilevered structure, the strongest point is nearest the building. If you are in any doubt about the load-bearing potential of your balcony, consult a qualified surveyor. Reduce weight with plastic or fibreglass planters and lightweight potting mixtures.

Inspirations

Careful planning and inspired planting can make the smallest balcony a space to relax and enjoy the open air. Semi-circular tables are ideal for dining al fresco where space is limited and can even be hinged to the wall or balcony railings and folded away when not required.

PLANTING TRICKS

To gain extra growing space, think vertical. Plants that grow to differing heights will provide more interest than varieties that tend to bush and the taller plants will provide valuable shade for the lower ones. Climbing and trailing plants add greatly to the effect and take up the minimum amount of precious floor space. Run trellis up any available wall, hang baskets on brackets and place troughs on window sills. Only fix planters to balcony rails if you are absolutely sure it is safe to do so.

GARDEN WISDOM

Balconies can be enjoyed from the street as well as from inside your home. Bold colour schemes are more effective in confined growing spaces, especially when viewed from a distance. You could decide to pick two or three colours or concentrate on just one for a really striking display. Think of your balcony as an extension of the room and choose containers and furnishings that echo the general style of your home. Do remember that any containers or furniture on your balcony must be firmly secured.

Inspirations

Foliage plants, small potted trees and bushes, heathers and ornamental cabbages will give interest at different times of the year. You can easily augment them with seasonal flowering plants such as winter pansies and daffodils. There are many attractive plastic planters available that will save you weight.

THE PLANTS

Acer
Calluna (Heather)
Cotoneaster
Hosta
Miscanthus
Pelargonium
Pyracantha
Sinarundinaria

dizzy heights

LIVING IN TOWN CAN OFTEN MEAN sacrificing the pleasures of outdoor life that a garden gives. However, enterprising people have realised that the roof garden can be one of the most delightful of all small gardens. The first things to think about with any roof garden are access and structural integrity. Flat roofs are designed to support heavy loads, however it is vital to check with a structural engineer exactly what the load bearing capacity of your roof is before you begin. Clearly define the boundaries, make sure the edges of the roof are securely railed especially if you intend using your terrace at night.

TIMESAVER

When you are planning your roof terrace think about having a water tap plumbed in. Roof tops can be very exposed to the elements and you will need to water your plants more often than if they were growing at ground level. Countless trips up and down stairs with your watering can will spoil your enjoyment.

GROUND RULES

Roof gardens will often experience extremes of temperature and can be very windswept. They are not the place for delicate plants or flowers. Try to break up the space with wooden pergolas, arbours or trellises. This will make the area more visually attractive while providing shade and shelter for less hardy plants. Remember that safety is always a consideration with roof gardens so be sure that any structure is securely fixed to the floor.

THE PLANTS

Armeria (Thrift)
Clematis
Impatiens (Busy Lizzie)
Lobelia
Nicotiana (Tobacco Plant)
Petunia
Rosa (Roses)
Tropaeolum (Nasturtium)

Inspirations

Eclectic groupings of flowering and foliage plants, climbers and bushes give the informal atmosphere and variety important for roof terraces. Cover the top soil of pots with gravel or pebbles to conserve moisture and prevent the wind blowing the earth away.

PLANTING TRICKS

A roof garden is an ideal space to use throughout the year so make sure you have a variety of plants that will provide pleasure in winter as well as summer. Roof gardening will almost certainly be container gardening so choose a variety of weatherproof containers. Break up the flatness of your terrace by choosing hardy plants of differing heights. Remember that a large glazed pot full of damp earth with an established plant can be surprisingly heavy.

Inspirations

One of the most interesting features of a roof terrace is the roof scape that surrounds it so beware of blocking the view by overplanting. The combination of textures and colours of roof tiles, bricks and plants can be inspirational, but be careful that climbing or trailing plants do not block gutters.

the outdoor dining room

AMONG THE GREATEST PLEASURES that you can experience in your garden are a lazy lunch with friends and dining out under the stars on a warm evening. Eating in the open air is always special whether it is a relaxed breakfast, or a full-scale feast. With a little thought you can easily create a dining area that you can use during warmer months. Of course, as well as using your garden as an outside dining room, it is also possible to cook outdoors. There are few more social ways to entertain than a barbecue, especially when you have designed an area specifically for this purpose. Food always tastes better outdoors so, no matter how limited space may be, dedicating an area in your garden for cooking and eating is always an excellent idea.

TIMESAVER

Where space is limited, choose weather-proof furniture that can be left outside all year. When you wish to eat in the garden, simply add a colourful tablecloth – and seat cushions for comfort. Cast iron furniture makes an attractive addition to almost any setting throughout the year and requires minimal maintenance.

PLANTING TRICKS

When planning dining areas, remember that eating in full sunlight is uncomfortable. Pick a shady part of the garden, arrange your table under a pergola or use free-standing sunshades.

Scented plants, such as rosemary or thyme, can add to the appeal of dining out of doors but very strong fragrances can sometimes be unappetising.

Eating out at night is a magical experience. Even if you have garden lighting, use candles, oil lamps or flambeaux to create a more intimate atmosphere. Specially scented garden candles will discourage those annoying flying insects that can disrupt an 'al fresco' meal.

Inspirations

An all-weather table can quickly be converted into a dining area with the addition of folding directors' chairs, which can be stored indoors. Simple table settings are all that is needed and plant stands placed nearby give colour and height while helping to define the dining area.

THE PLANTS

Dianthus (Pinks)
Jasminum (Jasmine)
Lavandula (Lavender)
Lobelia
Nicotiana (Tobacco Plant)
Nigella (Love-in-a-Mist)
Pelargonium (Ivy Leaved)
Rosa (Roses)

scent at night

EVEN WHEN THE HEAT OF THE DAY is over you can still enjoy the wonderful scent of aromatic herbs and sweet-smelling plants at night. Create a scented area on your patio but ease the strain of moving heavy plant pots with either a commercially available plant pot wheel base or by creating a simple trough on wheels with casters attached to a wooden crate. Choose a range of herbs like rosemary, sage and lavender and complement their aromatic scent with the lighter floral tones of jasmine and plumbago. Then just sit back, relax and enjoy their soothing scent.

YOU WILL NEED

medium glass paper
a sturdy wooden crate or box
1 litre of exterior undercoat
1 litre of exterior matt
    emulsion
polyeurethane matt varnish
paint brushes
four casters with appropriate
    sized screws
screwdriver

STEP 1

Using medium glass paper sand any rough edges from the box. Apply an even coat of undercoat and leave to dry. Apply one or more top coats as necessary. Finish with a coat of matt varnish. When completely dry, turn the box upside down and screw the four casters firmly to the corners. Ensure that the screws do not protrude through to the inside of the box.

THE PLANTS

Rosmarinus (Rosemary)
Variegated Hebe
Sage
Jasminum (Jasmine)
Lavandula (Lavender)
Plumbago
Hydrangea

STEP 2

Gently place the potted plants inside the box and wheel it to the desired locations. This will also work on some lawns, provided the ground is not too soft. You can buy similar commercially available wheel bases for your plant pots, though you may need several as they are usually only sufficient for one pot at a time.

    For a spectacular display, choose plants of different heights and arrange them in order of height with the tallest furthest away. This will mean that the scent from smaller plants will not be blocked by larger plants.

dry underfoot

THE FEEL OF SPRINGY GRASS UNDERFOOT is fine on a dry summer's day, but not so attractive in winter when lawns can rapidly become muddy no-go areas. To enjoy those crisp, clear winter mornings and bright spring days, you will need to make sure there are at least some parts of your garden that have all-weather surfaces. These will encourage you to venture out without the risk of bringing the garden into the house on the soles of your feet. There are many types of practical and attractive surfaces that can transform parts, if not all, of your garden into an outside room for all seasons. A terrace or patio near your house makes using your garden in winter a much more appealing proposition.

GROUND RULES
There are many all-weather surfaces that can be laid in the garden. Gravel, paving and decking are the most commonly used materials but pebbles set in cement, mosaic, bricks and tiles can all make interesting and durable surfaces. A mixture of materials can look particularly effective but plan the design carefully so that you get a subtle blend of textures. Do check that any materials you choose are frost-proof and suitable for exterior use.

GARDEN WISDOM
Gravel is perhaps the least expensive and most versatile of all-weather surfaces if laid and maintained correctly. It is available in a range of colours and should be laid about 10–15 cm deep, and should be raked regularly to discourage weeds. However, you can, if you wish, deliberately grow plants in gravel. The stones will rapidly disappear into other parts of the garden if they do not have proper edging to contain them. Choose edging that contrasts with the colour of the gravel.

Inspirations
Wooden decking always looks great and can evoke the languor and elegance of colonial living. Soften the edges of the deck and integrate it into the rest of the garden with densely planted borders. Decking can, however, be expensive, needs professional fitting and can be slippery when wet.

TIMESAVER

Many stone and wood surfaces change colour when wet and can become very slippery in the rain. Before you commit yourself, take a sample home and leave it in the garden for a few days. It's too late after you've laid the surface to find it is dangerous or unattractive after rain.

Inspirations

Designs in floor surfaces, like this radial motif, can create focal points in your garden. Choose your site carefully: sheltered spots with lots of sun are ideal. You can add screening – and some shade if necessary – to make a practical year-round retreat that will give you pleasure whatever the season.

THE PLANTS

Allium (Chives)
Armeria
Begonia
Cordyline
Rosa (Roses)
Salvia (Sage)
Thymus (Thyme)
Tropaeolum (Nasturtium)

light at night

JUST AS YOU CAN DESIGN YOUR GARDEN to become an outside room, adding lighting extends the time you can enjoy relaxing, eating and socialising in this space. Lighting can be used in three different ways in the garden. Landscape lighting: highlights attractive areas of your garden, giving it depth at night. Task lighting: illuminates areas you will want to use after dark – patios and paths for example. Use security lighting to deter intruders and provide extremely bright general lighting. Make your garden an intriguing and magical place to be after dark, especially during the autumn and winter months.

Inspirations

Galvanised lanterns and candle holders can provide an interesting and practical contrast to the soft, colourful textures of your garden. Candles provide a softer, more interesting light than electric fittings and you can move them easily to create a variety of effects. Be aware of the risk of fire and keep an extinguisher handy.

LIGHTING TRICKS

Don't stop at simply lighting your patio or barbecue area, leaving the rest of the garden in darkness. Just a few lights carefully positioned can create the illusion of space and will make a wonderful backdrop to your 'al fresco meal'. Use lower wattage lighting towards the end of the garden to give an impression of depth. Up-lighting plants through their foliage will emphasise any movement on balmy nights and create interesting patterns.

TIMESAVER

You don't have to pay for an extensive electrical installation to enjoy lighting in your garden. Consider candles and flambeaux – which can have the added advantage of discouraging flying insects at night. If breezy, put candles in lanterns or under shades to prevent them blowing out.

GROUND RULES

Whatever type of lighting you decide on, beware of glare. Task lighting will have little effect if it dazzles. Keep bright lighting for security and create atmosphere by using lower power levels elsewhere. Try at night and you'll be surprised at how little light you need to create an impressive effect. Make sure you are aware of the effect rather than the source of the light.

Inspirations

Highlighting elements of your garden can bring out the vivid colour of a display of flowering plants, allowing them to be enjoyed long after the sun has set. You can also spotlight focal points such as statues and fountains. Some light fittings get hot so be careful not to scorch your plants.

THE PLANTS

Buxus (Box)
Chrysanthemum (Marguerite)
Gladiolus
Hyacinthus (Hyacinth)
Lavandula (Lavender)
Nicotiana (Tobacco Plant)
Petunia
Rosa (Roses)

edible garden

IF YOU ARE A KEEN COOK AND GARDENER but do not have the time or the space for a gourmet garden, then either a hanging basket of herbs or pots planted with herbs and vegetables are the answer. Fresh herbs in cooking enhance the presentation, flavour and aroma of the food. Culinary herbs are simple to grow from seed or can be bought ready potted. They are easy to maintain and brighten up window sills, hanging baskets or plant stands. Make sure when choosing herbs for your hanging basket, that the plants will grow well together sharing the same conditions and plant care routines.

HANGING BASKET

Before planting your herb basket cut some capillary or plastic liner to the size of your basket, fill the basket with compost to just below the top of the the liner. Arrange the plants with the tallest at the centre of the basket, smaller ones towards the edge. Fill any gaps between the plants with compost.

Hang your basket in your chosen position. Position the basket so that it is easy to water, preferably not above eye level. Ensure that any bracket or fixing is strong and secure. If attaching the basket to a wall, drill a hole with a masonry bit, plug with a rawl plug and insert the hook.

YOU WILL NEED

1 trowel
basket lining material
1 basket
general purpose light weight compost
fixings

THE PLANTS

Gold Curled Marjoram
Silver Posie Thyme
Broad-leaved Thyme
Chives
Parsley
Thyme Doone Valley
Rosmarinus (Rosemary)

Inspirations

When the herbs are mature harvest them to preserve and dry for when they are no longer available. Pick the herbs when they are at their peak and full of flavour, tie the stalks lightly and hang them upside down in a warm, dry, dark place. Some herbs like mint and coriander can also be frozen.

INDIVIDUAL HERBS AND VEGETABLES

This plant stand is ideal for growing and displaying herbs and vegetables. The pots can be moved around for ripening in the sun. The stand itself can be moved easily and the plantings can be interspersed with decorative plants like geraniums and pelargoniums. An interesting alternative would be tiered pots of crops such as ornamental cabbages, tomatoes, and peppers.

THE PLANTS

Mint
Parsley
Rosmarinus (Rosemary)
Salvia (Sage)
Strawberry

Special features give a garden added perspective, creating exciting visual interest. Some features are part of the landscape – for example sloping ground or a steep embankment at the end of your garden – and cannot be ignored. A raised terrace or rockery can turn difficult features into assets.

FOCUS ON FEATURES

There are many ways to add new dimensions to your outdoor spaces. Concentrate on just one or two features and make them really special.

tiered wall garden

SINCE PEOPLE FIRST STARTED CULTIVATING THE LAND, sloping ground has presented us with a number of problems, most of which can be overcome by terracing. Most domestic gardens are on level ground, however some houses are built on sites where there is no alternative but to site the garden – or at least part of it – on sloping ground. In these situations, terracing not only provides a solution but also forms a natural windbreak. Furthermore, the retaining walls absorb warmth on sunny days, which can promote more rapid plant growth.

PLANTING TRICKS

Terracing your garden is a major undertaking so make sure you have examined the other possibilities. If it isn't too steep, you could turn the area into a rockery or simply turf it over and plant it with bulbs. Alternatively, rather than fully terracing a slope, you could simply create a level area at the top and cut some steps up to it. This will give you a private secluded area with an elevated view of the garden.

GROUND RULES

Terracing prevents valuable topsoil being washed downhill. When cutting terraces remove the topsoil first and put to one side. Replace this soil on the new beds created by the terraces. You can create terraces in flatter gardens by excavating one part and using the soil to make raised areas elsewhere.

Inspirations

If you have to terrace part of your garden then turn necessity to your advantage and create a cascade of colour. Well-designed terraces can achieve a density of planting with which the level garden simply cannot compete. Terraces do not have to be solely for planting but can also be used to provide areas for seating.

GARDEN WISDOM

The retaining walls of terraces must be well constructed as they have to support a substantial weight. If you use wood rather than brick or concrete for your walls, make absolutely sure it has been treated against rot. Recycled railway sleepers are virtually indestructible and relatively inexpensive.

PLANTING TRICKS

Terraces give a fantastic opportunity to vary your planting. You could treat each level as a separate garden: grow herbs on one level, alpines on another or simply gravel a terrace and use it as a platform for container planting. The possibilities are limitless.

THE PLANTS

Delphinium

Genista

Nepeta (Catmint)

Parahebe

Pelargonium

Petunia

Rosa (Roses)

Sidalcea

sitting pretty

LIKE ANY ROOM IN YOUR HOUSE, your garden needs furnishing. You will almost certainly want to provide somewhere to sit and perhaps a table for eating outdoors on sunny days. Garden furniture can be divided into two types: furniture that is only taken out when needed and has to be protected from the elements and furniture that is permanent and durable enough to live outside all year. Removable furniture can easily be bought but you will need somewhere dry to store it when not in use. Durable furniture will become a year-round feature in your garden so it will need to be chosen very carefully.

GROUND RULES

Your garden furniture should complement the general style of your garden be it classical, formal, rustic, cottage, oriental or modern minimal. As a rule, toning colours work best: white, green, black or natural wood for example. Colour and contrast can be introduced with patterned fabrics, cushions and tablecloths. Position your furniture carefully in relation to other garden features and consider the position of the sun throughout the day.

TIMESAVER

As well as looking for furniture in garden centres, you can often pick up handsome iron chairs and rustic benches in junk shops or auction sales. Don't worry if your finds are not in pristine condition. As long as it is structurally sound, garden furniture looks better weathered.

Inspirations

Placed against a wall for shelter, a bench surrounded by plants creates a perfect suntrap and invites you to sit and enjoy the garden. Fragrant plants such as lavender or herbs planted nearby will provide a further sensual treat. Garden furniture can also look extremely effective framed by colourful flowering creepers and planted containers.

THE PLANTS

Anethum (Dill)
Digitalis (Foxglove)
Mentha (Mint)
Nepeta (Catmint)
Rosmarinus (Rosemary)
Salvia (Sage)
Tropaeolum (Nasturtium)

water features

THERE CAN BE FEW SOUNDS AS IMMEDIATELY SOOTHING as moving water. Even the sound of birds happily splashing in a bird bath can add enormously to the enjoyment of your garden. Introducing water features will not only bring variety but an unequalled sense of tranquillity. The play of light on water and its constantly changing form introduces a delightful extra dimension to your garden and has the added advantage of attracting a variety of wildlife. No matter how small your garden there is a way to introduce water, that most vital of elements, into your total scheme.

GROUND RULES

Siting of water features is an important consideration. If the water is not constantly moving, algae will quickly form in pools situated in the sunniest part of the garden. Fish will also appreciate a little shade. Pools positioned directly under deciduous trees will result in autumns spent constantly raking out leaves. Ideally, water features should be planned and installed before the rest of the garden is planted, as any plumbing or electrical installation will cause disruption later. Always use a qualified electrician for any electrical work.

Inspirations

Simple stylised water features can bring both the sound and sight of moving water into your garden without taking up huge amounts of space. Water courses inspired by Japanese Zen gardens will bring added interest and style to container plantings and are simple to install with minimal disturbance.

TIMESAVER

Moving water does not have to involve complicated plumbing. Recycling pumps can create the effect of natural running water. Complete kits are available for ornamental wall-mounted fountains where water constantly trickles from a spout into a bowl below. Always seek specialist advice on installation.

PLANTING TRICKS

Many water plants grow vigorously and can spread quickly, engulfing their more sedate neighbours. You can control growth either by regular thinning out or by planting in specially designed plastic mesh containers that inhibit root growth and prevent soil becoming waterlogged and stagnant. Raise up young plants such as water lilies, on bricks or plastic plinths. Adjust these as the plants grow, until they reach their ideal planting depth.

Inspirations

A quiet shady corner of the garden is an ideal place for a water feature. Basins can be particularly effective in patio gardens. You can create fascinating contrasts of texture with this type of feature. When choosing the site, consider the way sunlight will fall on the water at different times of the day.

THE PLANTS

Acorus (Sweet Flag)
Caltha (Marsh Marigold)
Hosta (Plantain Lily)
Iris (Yellow Flag)
Lemna (Duckweed)
Nymphaea (Water Lily)
Persicaria (Bistort)
Sagittaria

water garden

ADD A TOUCH OF DRAMA to your garden with water. If you are lucky enough to have a pond, make the most of it with beautiful lilies and lush green rushes. Alternatively, it is easy to make an attractive miniature water garden. This water garden is also an ideal way to bring the outdoors inside, it can be as simple or as elaborate as you like, but it is important to change the water regularly. In the background of the main picture a bamboo plant is kept in a blue lustre glaze pot, the shiny blue of the pot reflects the light and complements the water garden.

YOU WILL NEED
1 large ceramic bowl
water
stones and pebbles

PLANTING TRICKS
A water garden is a decorative yet tranquil garden feature. If you have lots of room go wild and indulge yourself with a large water garden full of beautiful lilies, irises and rushes.
A water garden is guaranteed to enhance the beauty of any outside area.

THE PLANTS

Anemone
Juncus inflexus
Lavatera
Nymphaea (Water Lily)
Salvia variegata (Variegated Sage)

STEP ONE
To make this water garden, simply fill a large ceramic bowl with water. Add a selection of waterplants, in this case Juncus inflexus and Lavatera. Keep the plants in their pots so that the soil is not washed away, they will still be able to draw water in from their base.

STEP TWO
Add water to the bowl, but keep it just below the level of the pots or the water will become muddy. If you prefer to disguise the pots, cover and surround them with stones and pebbles – these will look particularly attractive when wet.

the wild side

THE ROMANCE OF A WALK through a bluebell wood in springtime, a field full of poppies in the middle of summer or simply the beauty of a hedgerow in autumn are a very special part of our natural heritage. In all but the very smallest gardens it is possible to introduce an element of the wilderness. An old 'Belfast' sink planted with a profusion of wild flowers can create an eyecatching effect. In the planned and controlled environment of the urban garden, don't mistake wilderness gardening for no-maintenance gardening. The wild garden will only succeed with careful planning and constant attention.

PLANTING TRICKS

To create a genuine natural wilderness garden, you must do some investigating. Find out which plants are actually growing wild near you. This way you will find varieties suited to the local growing conditions and climate. Although you should never uproot plants growing wild, it is acceptable to collect seeds. Plant native trees and shrubs rather than being tempted by foreign varieties, with the exception of the buddleia or butterfly bush. Wild flowers have survived because they grow vigorously and spread rapidly. Nature cannot be allowed to run riot in the garden or it will rapidly choke the more delicate plants we take so much care to nurture. However, maintenance of wilderness areas is more informal than other parts of the garden. Meadow lawns, for example, need mowing with a scythe no more than twice a year.

Inspirations

Dense planting and careful maintenance are needed to create an overgrown effect. An amazing variety of wild flowers will flourish in a very small area, creating an effect of which only nature is capable. A simple packet of wild flower seeds can produce a riot of colour and texture.

TIMESAVER

If you are considering planting a wild meadow, mix your wild flower seeds with the grass seeds before sowing. If you sow wild flower seeds in established grass it will stifle their growth. To add more later, cut out patches of grass and plant established flowers.

GARDEN WISDOM

Beware of making paths too straight or the effect will look contrived. Mow meandering tracks through meadow grass or use weathered stepping stones. Paths don't have to lead anywhere but can give the illusion of greater length as they disappear around a corner.

PLANTING TRICKS

Wild areas in gardens can rapidly become home to a variety of animals and birds and you can gain great enjoyment from simply observing them in a more natural habitat. Put feeders in a sheltered spot near shrubs and bushes where birds can perch and to which they can retreat if disturbed. Wild plants often prefer poorer quality soil and will grow more abundantly if you remove the top 10cm of earth before planting your wild garden.

Inspirations

Bark chippings are a natural-looking way to define paths in wilderness areas and help prevent the ground becoming overgrown. One of the great joys of natural plantings is their sheer exuberance and an element of encroachment is to be encouraged. Wild plants grow in a remarkable variety of colours and heights, giving a timeless sense of the countryside.

THE PLANTS

Alyssum
Aubrieta
Campanula carpatica
Dianthus deltoides
Helianthemum
Phlox caespitosa
Thymus varieties e.g.
lemon-scented thyme

rocks and rockeries

INTREPID VICTORIAN MOUNTAINEERS tackling alpine summits became entranced by hardy little plants flowering colourfully in the inhospitable cracks and crevices of the mountain rocks. So began the English fascination with alpine plants and creating rockeries on which to grow them. Today rockeries can be planted with all kinds of rock plants, many much less demanding of full sunlight than true alpines like edelweiss and gentian. Rockeries can be expensive and are hard work to maintain, but there are simple ways to introduce an 'alpine' theme.

PLANTING TRICKS

True alpine plants demand lots of sun and need a well-drained site as they will soon fail if they become waterlogged. However there are many rock plants that will thrive in shadier or damper conditions and still give the effect of an alpine rockery. Primulas, dwarf bamboos and some dwarf conifers for example, which are happy in damp conditions, can be grown to great effect among rocks. Alpine plants can also be grown in sunny well-drained 'scree' beds.

Inspirations
What can be more inspiring than hardy little alpine plants cheerfully growing in seemingly inhospitable conditions? Most true alpines flower in the spring (when the snow has just melted) so look for other plants like heathers and conifers to provide interest at other times of the year.

TIMESAVER
Create miniature alpine displays in stone troughs. Alternatively, you can coat an old-fashioned Belfast sink with a mixture of sand, cement and peat to give a convincing stone finish. Make sure you have your trough or sink in its final position before you begin planting.

GROUND RULES

The most important thing about rockeries is the rocks. Don't be tempted to substitute builders' rubble because that is exactly what it will end up looking like. True rock garden stones can weigh between 100 and 200 kilos and are expensive but look wonderful and will weather marvellously. Check that your supplier will deliver.

Inspirations

A variety of flowering plants, shrubs and heathers grouped around a central display will provide exquisite pleasure throughout the year. In the winter the lichen-covered stones make a fascinating display in their own right. Good drainage and a sunny position are essential in a scheme like this.

THE PLANTS

Alyssum
Aubrieta
Gentiana (Gentian)
Geranium (Cranesbill)
Leontopodium (Eidelweiss)
Saxifraga (Saxifrage)
Sempervivum (Houseleek)
Tropaeolum (Nasturtium)

edging

ADD DEFINITION TO YOUR GARDEN BORDERS with clever use of edging. You can use shells, rope, ornamental flower pots or bricks, the choice is only limited by your imagination. Edging is not only an attractive garden feature, but in some cases can also help to maintain a neat lawn edge. It can act as a frame to your borders and the russet colours of bricks, for example, can contrast beautifully with the green of your plants and the more vibrant colours of their flowers. It is not necessary to add edging around all the borders in your garden, if you prefer just frame your favourite area.

EDGE 1
You can easily achieve this very attractive edging by potting ornamental plants into small terracotta pots, and placing them along the edge of your grass, this has the effect of separating the lawn from the flower bed in a more unusual way.

EDGE 2
Rope is another effective edging. Here it is used to edge a path, combined with gravel, pebbles and rockery plants to add character to the garden. Chandlers' rope which is pretreated can be bought at hardware outlets. Fix the rope down using tent pegs or galvanized garden staples.

EDGE 3
For this edging scallop shells have been used, however it is possibe to use a variety of shells. You can collect these from the seashore, buy them in a department store or even ask for them at the fishmonger's. Simply push the shells into the soil, creating a border around your flower garden.

EDGE 4
Bricks can be bought very cheaply from reclamation centres, it is not necessary to buy them new. If you do not have bricks, you can improvise with stones. Simply push the bricks into the soil, edge to edge. Alternatively you can lay them on the narrow edge or cut them in half and lay them at an angle.

YOU WILL NEED
small potted plants
chandlers' rope
shells
red bricks

secret places

ALL REALLY MEMORABLE GARDENS have an air of mystery about them. The garden that reveals all its secrets at first glance does not hold our interest for long. The delight in coming upon an unexpected little corner, screened from the rest of the world, is one of the great joys of the well-planned garden. You can produce secret places even in the smallest of gardens, creating overgrown or shady little spots that can be enjoyed by young and old alike.

PLANTING TRICKS

Dark corners, previously overlooked, can be excellent places to produce secret corners. Most types of fern are happy growing in the shade and there is something mysterious about their luxuriant fronds. Don't worry if your secret place is in a damp part of the garden. Perhaps the most magical of secret places is the grotto, where dampness is part of the charm. Stone is a practical choice for seating in this kind of environment.

Inspirations

Overgrown plants and rough-cast stone flooring can contribute to the sense of controlled neglect that is an integral part of secret places in the garden. You can accentuate the atmosphere of the forgotten or overlooked space by siting a piece of weathered statuary so you don't discover it until the last moment.

GARDEN WISDOM

The wilderness garden is one of the most compelling situations for a secret place. Winding overgrown paths that quickly disappear from view lead enticingly to unseen delights. When glimpsed through a gate, a prospect like this creates an invitation to explore that is almost impossible to resist.

THE PLANTS

Begonia
Centaurea (Cornflower)
Cleome (Spider Flower)
Dryopteris (Fern)
Hyacinthus (Hyacinth)
Impatiens (Busy Lizzie)
Papaver (Poppy)
Rosa (Climbing Rose)

IDEAS

Specially designed secret places can be safe exploring areas for young children and will provide wonderful source material for their fertile imaginations.

Secret places are great for grown-ups too. An arbour in a shady corner can be a place of delightful retreat bedecked with hanging baskets and surrounded with lush foliage.

Inspirations

The promise of a secret place can be almost as intriguing as the spot itself. Who knows where this path may lead – perhaps nowhere – but it makes a wonderful vista.

arbours and bowers

WHAT MORE ROMANTIC FEATURE is there than the arbour, that quiet place of retreat both sheltered and yet open to the joys of your garden? Arbours can trace their origins back to ancient Egypt and Rome, where a shelter from dusty desert winds and the heat of the midday sun was a prerequisite of any established garden. Strictly speaking, an arbour is a shady retreat with sides and roof formed principally by trees or climbing plants. The modern arbour, however, can be any open-sided shelter and there are a great variety of styles to choose from.

TIMESAVER

You can buy prefabricated arbours from any large garden centre. Most are constructed of wood or thick wire. Like all structures designed to support plants, they must be robust. If you wish to make an arbour, it can be a simple construction. Stout posts with trellis walls supporting a pantiled roof make a delightfully mysterious retreat.

THE PLANTS

Clematis
Fuchsia
Hedera (Ivy)
Hydrangea
Lavatera (Mallow)
Polygonum (Russian Vine)
Rosa (Climbing Rose)

GROUND RULES

Two things are central to an arbour: a seat and a view. As well as places to shelter from the heat of the day or the vagaries of the climate, arbours are places to sit comfortably and enjoy your garden. Make sure to site your arbour so you get a good view.
Your arbour can be an impressive and decorative focal point. Choose a style that suits the scale and design of the rest of your garden.

PLANTING TRICKS

If space is really at a premium, site an arch against a wall and train clematis or honeysuckle over it. Add a small cast iron or wooden seat. This is a simple way to create the essence of an arbour and produce a really stunning effect in a small area.

Inspirations

The classic English bower – another name for an arbour – is a frame overgrown with rambling and climbing roses. This makes a truly delightful setting for a garden seat.

hanging gardens

IN ANY GARDEN, VARIETY IS IMPORTANT. In a small space this can be achieved by creating different levels and perspectives to interest the eye and provide the maximum area for planting. Vertical and trailing displays can be among the most spectacular ways to add a new dimension to your garden. Plants can be grown on trellises or netting fixed to walls but these tend to occur at the boundaries of the garden. Free-standing structures such as pergolas and arches provide an opportunity to introduce instant new perspectives, natural shade and visual punctuation to your general scheme.

PLANTING TRICKS
Your choice of pergola or arch will be decided by the type of plants you intend to grow over it. Plants such as wisteria and laburnum can be extremely heavy as they grow to maturity and will require substantial structures. Roses, clematis and honeysuckle are less heavy, while sweet-pea and morning glory will only require light support. Whatever type of structure you use, it is important to make sure it is securely anchored into the ground.

TIMESAVER
Arches or pergolas can be bought easily ready-to-assemble from larger garden centres. These features have immediate impact, so while plants are establishing themselves the structure is much more apparent, so match the style to the rest of the garden.

Inspirations
Rose arches across a path or framing part of a patio are the essence of the English country garden. Artfully overgrown trailing plants on a pergola give a more Mediterranean feel. Canopies of cascading foliage can be mirrored in wall baskets and ground level containers.

GARDEN WISDOM

Pergolas and arches can be made of various materials. Hardwood is more durable, and preferable to treated softwood. Brick piers with horizontal wires make an elegant architectural feature. Wire arches can be particularly useful for framing vistas or drawing the eye towards decorative features such as sun-dials, statues or ornamental trees. Constructing a pergola between the gate and the front door can completely transform a front garden. Add fragrant climbing plants.

Inspirations

Arches and pergolas planted with a profusion of climbing roses create a romantic frothy effect that would not be possible to achieve any other way. You can use arches to frame particular parts of the garden, to give perspective or simply to provide areas of dappled shade to sit in and relax, in the heat of the day.

THE PLANTS

Ceanothus
Clematis
Hedera (Ivy)
Humulus (Hop)
Lonicera (Honeysuckle)
Rosa (Rambling Rose)
Vitis (Grape Vine)
Wisteria

The introduction of a themed garden can be the ultimate expression of your interest and gardening skills. Many people choose to reserve part of their garden for the scent and variety of herbs, others seek the tranquility of a Japanese stone garden or the serenity of a garden with one type or colour of

THEMES AND SCHEMES

plant. Raised beds can add visual interest and are practical for access and to reduce bending. Massed plantings of one or two colours can make a bold impressive display in even the smallest space.

colour themes

AS WITH THE ROOMS IN YOUR HOUSE, you might find it valuable to devise a colour scheme for your garden. Some styles – the cottage garden and the wilderness garden, for example – rely on an assortment of random colours for their effect. However, once you decide on a more formal approach to your garden style, you will need to give some thought to the general effect your planting will produce. One very popular way to theme areas of your garden is to colour-group them. This involves picking one, or maybe two, colours for all the plants in one area.

PLANTING TRICKS

The most popular single colour to choose for colour theming is white. There is a huge range of white flowers. White roses, mock orange, marguerites, lilies, white lupins, white hydrangeas and Japanese anemones are just a few of the more common varieties. These blooms always look good against grey, silver or green foliage. Whatever your growing conditions, there will be a wide enough choice to produce a stunning display.

Inspirations

Single colour groupings can look both elegant and understated especially in a setting such as this where the white furniture, railings and containers further enhance the effect. Clipped box trees add a contrasting colour and underline the formal symmetry of the display.

GARDEN WISDOM

To make a really bold statement, stick with one colour. If you find this approach a little minimal, try two colours together, combining them with foliage plants for the best effect. Colour can create a powerful mood so choose with care.

PLANTING TRICKS

There are a great many shades of blue and purple that mix well with white, as well as looking wonderful on their own. Herbs such as lavender, flax, rosemary and sage have delicate blue flowers which, when combined with cornflowers, delphiniums, speedwell and viburnum, can make a display that looks and smells unforgettable.

Inspirations

Red trailing pelargoniums massed in hanging baskets and spilling out of containers give a typically Gallic feel to this flagstoned courtyard. Red plants alone can be overpowering so small beds have been planted with white pelargoniums for variety. Pelargoniums are generally hardy plants requiring the minimum of attention for the maximum effect.

THE PLANTS

Artemisia
Buxus (Box)
Chrysanthemum
Hydrangea
Lobelia
Paeonia (Peony)
Pelargonium
Petunia

raised beds

THE TOWN GARDEN is often a level, symmetrical space. Changes of level in the garden break up the horizon and make for greater diversity. Raised beds are perfect for giving a varied look to the actual shape of your garden. They can form natural divisions, creating discreet areas that break up the potential monotony of the rectangular or square garden. Raised beds are normally permanent structures and, if sympathetically designed and built, can bring a sense of maturity and permanence to a garden that is only just becoming established. For planting purposes, consider them as giant, permanent containers.

GROUND RULES

Railway sleepers make attractive and durable retaining walls for raised beds. Designed to be extremely hard wearing, they should last for many years in your garden. This is also an ecologically aware use of resources.

Inspirations

You can make raised beds from a variety of materials but remember to provide 'weep holes' for drainage. Line concrete or brick with plastic if planting lime-haters such as rhododendrons.

TIMESAVER

An ideal height for raised beds is between 45 and 60 cm. This will not only have the best visual impact but will make gardening much more comfortable. For ease of maintenance, don't make the beds too deep from front to back.

PLANTING TRICKS

Raised beds have several practical advantages. In areas of poor soil they provide a controllable area in which the planting environment can be carefully created and maintained. Because the soil can be easily varied from bed to bed, plants that require different types of soil or different growing conditions can be introduced close to each other, providing unusual displays. The retaining walls of raised beds can be attractive features in themselves and can form an interesting backdrop to climbing or trailing plants.

GARDEN WISDOM

When building raised beds, choose materials that are in sympathy with the construction of the house or other garden features. Lay a 25 to 30 cm layer of rubble inside for drainage then top up with a mix of good quality garden soil and compost. Finish off with a layer of bark chippings or coarse grit to deter weeds and retain moisture.

Inspirations

Painting retaining walls white will make a striking contrast with your planting and will bring extra light into your garden. Plant trailing plants near the edges of the beds and encourage them to cascade over the sides to add extra interest to the vertical surfaces.

THE PLANTS

Alchemilla
Digitalis (Foxgloves)
Fuchsia
Hedera (Ivy)
Hosta
Lobelia
Pelargoniums
Rosa (Roses)

rose garden

ROSES, COMMONLY REPRESENTED as the essence of Englishness, have in fact been enjoyed since before Roman times and are grown in many parts of the world. They have been a staple part of the English garden since the Middle Ages and more effort goes into breeding them than any other plant. It is hard to imagine an English garden without some kind of rose growing in it. There are so many different types and colours of roses available that there is sure to be one that is perfect for your garden. Well-tended roses will last for at least twenty years so you will be able enjoy them year after year.

PLANTING TRICKS

All roses require good quality soil and should not be planted in earth in which other roses have been growing. They need good drainage, plenty of sunshine and a moderately sheltered spot but do not grow them under trees. Roses require a lot of nutrients, so you need to have access to the soil around the roots for fertilising and mulching. A bit of mystique has grown up around rose growing, but the techniques required can be quickly learned. The rose, a true thoroughbred, will repay your efforts many times over.

GARDEN WISDOM

Although most roses are happiest growing in beds, the needs of the container gardener have not been forgotten. Patio roses (small floribunda bushes), give a wonderful display and come in a wide variety of flower types and colours. Miniature roses can be grown indoors and out, in pots, troughs or rockeries.

GARDEN WISDOM

There are many different sorts of roses available and it is important to understand the principal types. The standard rose, also known as the rose tree, is actually a long rigid stem with another rose grafted on top. Floribundas bloom in clusters, giving long lasting displays with lots of colour. Although most types of shrub rose flower only once, they are a good choice for beginners as they require little attention and have impressively large blooms.

Inspirations

There really is a rose for every situation. Climbing roses trail up trellises and over arches, producing spectacular clusters of flowers. Bush roses produce easy-to-maintain displays of massed blooms throughout the summer, while standard roses lend a formal air and give instant height to your display. There are many specialist growers who produce lavishly illustrated catalogues of roses for you to browse through over the winter months.

PLANTING TRICKS

It is important to understand the difference between climbing and rambling roses. Climbing roses have rigid stems, flower for long periods and are typically grown up pergolas, trellises and arches. Rambling roses have pliable bramble-like stems, flower only once, need hard pruning and are best avoided by beginner gardeners.

Inspirations

It is easy to become intoxicated by rose growing and whole gardens can be completely dedicated to the many guises of this wonderfully rewarding plant. Roses tend to be grown either for their scent or for their bloom, so choose a selection of both for the complete sensual experience.

THE PLANTS

Rosa 'Anne Harkness' (Floribunda)
Rosa 'Compassion' (Climbing Rose)
Rosa 'Elina' (Hybrid Tea)
Rosa 'Flower Carpet' (Ground Cover Rose)
Rosa 'Pink Favourite' (Hybrid Tea)
Rosa rugosa 'Alba' (Shrub Rose)
Rosa rugosa 'Scrabrosa' (Shrub Rose)
Rosa 'Sweet Dream' (Patio Bush)

pebble and Japanese gardens

CALM, TRANQUILLITY, STILLNESS: these are the qualities of the Japanese garden. Your aim is to create a contemplative mood in a place where you can escape harsh reality and drift into an altogether more serene frame of mind. A dedication to simplicity and purity of style will help you achieve a pool of eastern tranquillity in your hectic western life. You can design your whole garden in the Japanese style or use just a corner to create the essence of Zen. Include simple water features and carefully arranged rocks, artfully raked gravel and plants chosen for the colour and texture of their leaves.

Inspirations

Japanese gardens should emphasise the carefully planned use of space. They should be designed to be looked at rather than walked through: a living picture to be contemplated. Low growing evergreens, Japanese maples, ferns and mosses have interesting shapes, colours and textures throughout the year. A few carefully-designed features will evoke the spirit of the Japanese garden in the smallest of spaces. Choose roughly-glazed containers, interesting foliage plants, a few stepping stones set in raked gravel and a weathered rock covered in lichen.

THE PLANTS

Acer
Carex (Sedge)
Festuca glauca
Phyllostachys pleioblastus
(Bamboo)
Sasa shibataea

GROUND RULES

Whatever the scale, a Japanese garden takes care and attention, but will need little weeding. Make sure your gravel is well drained and buy a rubber rake to keep those all-important patterns you have made looking good.

GARDEN WISDOM

Don't be too concerned with choosing plants for their flowers, but instead select them for their texture and colour. Plants are one element of the harmonious whole that is the Japanese garden but they should not overwhelm the complete design. Bamboo makes an effective backdrop but do remember to cut bamboo just above a join if possible so the end is solid and will not collect rainwater.

physic garden

ONE OF THE MOST ANCIENT FORMS OF GARDEN is the physic or herbal garden. Growing plants for medicinal, culinary, or cosmetic purposes has been practised for hundreds of years. Although there has always been a lively debate about the medicinal use of plants, there is no doubting the value of fresh herbs in cooking – and what fresher herbs than those from your own garden, balcony or window sill? As well as their practical uses, herbs have their own special kind of beauty and their scent can add a sensual dimension to any garden. There is a place for these aromatic plants in every garden.

GROUND RULES

Herbs are generally hardy plants but their soil requirements can vary. Mediterranean herbs such as thyme, bay, rosemary and sage prefer poor, well-drained soil. Adding lime to the mixture will help to reproduce their native environment. Mint, chives and other herbs that originated in wetter climates require rich, moist soil to thrive. Although most herbs need plenty of sunlight, strong winds can damage leaves and inhibit healthy growth.

Inspirations

Once grown just for their practical uses, herbs are now appreciated as attractive plants in their own right. Although they may not be as dramatic as other flowering plants, their subtly coloured leaves and typically blue, mauve or yellow flowers can make an attractive, and of course wonderfully aromatic, display.

TIMESAVER

It is possible to grow herbs from seed, though parsley is notoriously difficult. A quicker and easier, though more expensive, solution is to buy herbs in pots. Buy plants from a garden centre or herbalist. Potted herbs sold in supermarkets are cultivated for eating rather than planting.

PLANTING TRICKS

Herbs are especially suited to container planting. Larger herbs such as lavender and rosemary can be grown singly in large pots and can be trimmed into attractive shapes. Smaller herbs are better suited to mixed planting for the best effect. Strawberry pots can be adapted for use as herb planters, enabling you to grow several varieties in a small space. Remember mint spreads prolifically and is best planted by itself.

Inspirations

Most stately homes and monasteries will have a physic or herbal garden in the grounds. It is well worth visiting these beautiful gardens for inspiration. The Chelsea Physic Garden, for example, is an oasis of peace and tranquillity in the centre of London. Indeed, many herbal gardens have a very special atmosphere.

TIMESAVER

Most herbs will die back over winter if left outside. Dig up some healthy specimens in early autumn and re-pot them in fresh compost. Water well, trim off all but the healthiest leaves and place the plants on a sunny, draught-free window sill. Feed them occasionally and enjoy the wonderful taste of fresh herbs throughout the winter.

THE PLANTS

Borago (Borage)
Chamomile
Lavandula (Lavender)
Mentha (Mint)
Ocimum (Basil)
Petroselinum (Parsley)
Salvia (Sage)
Thymus (Thyme)

tools

GARDENING IS, FOR MOST PEOPLE, a pleasurable hobby and having the right tools for the job is part of that pleasure. Buy the best you can afford and, if necessary, build up your collection gradually. You must feel comfortable with your choice so, if possible, borrow tools from gardening friends first to try them out. Depending on the type of garden you have, you may not need all the tools in this list. If you haven't got a shed to store your tools in, you will at least need a lockable outdoor cupboard. Tools can be a danger to children and can be used by opportunist burglars to gain entry to your home so it is important to keep them shut away securely when not in use.

Well-chosen and cherished over the years, tools can also be very decorative and become part of the garden scheme. With a patina of age gained from many seasons of heavy use, these implements are almost too good to hide away in a shed.

THE TOOLS:

Garden spade: Stainless steel spades cut through the soil better than other types but are more expensive. Experienced gardeners say they are worth every penny. D-shaped handles are considered easier to grip than T-shaped versions. Wooden handles feel warm to the touch and can be replaced if they break. Always buy a spade that has a foot-tread on the top of the blade. This type is much more comfortable to use. Wipe over your spade before you put it away.

Garden fork: Choose from carbon steel or stainless steel. It doesn't make much difference as long as they are well-made. Forks come in different sizes. A smaller 'ladies' type may be all you need for a small garden.

Hoe: Good for weeding without having to bend down. Some people swear by Dutch hoes, others prefer the 'push-pull' type. Try both first to see which you find easier to use.

Rake: You need the sort with short tines (prongs) for breaking up lumps of soil and creating a smooth surface for planting and sowing. If you have this type of rake and a fork you are unlikely to need a cultivator. For clearing leaves and moss from lawns, buy the sort of rake that has long, springy wire tines.

Hand fork: For weeding around plants. Flat tines are best as they don't clog up. Long-handled versions are useful for reaching to the backs of beds and brightly coloured handles are handy for finding tools when you put them down amongst foliage.

Hand trowel: For planting smaller plants, where a spade is too large. As with spades, stainless steel is worth the investment. Buy a standard width trowel and a narrow one. Non-stick Teflon coatings are a good idea, especially for clay soil.

Wheelbarrow: Only really necessary for larger gardens, even then make sure you don't buy one that is bigger or heavier than you need. Remember you will have to store it somewhere. A large garden bag, called a 'tip' bag, may be sufficient.

Watering can or hosepipe: You don't necessarily need both and, with either, a handy garden tap makes life much easier. If you intend to leave a watering can on display, choose an attractive metal one, otherwise buy a medium-priced one made from plastic. If you buy a hose make sure that it is long enough and the coupling is the right one for your tap. Braided hose is less likely to kink. You can also buy accessories for your hose, such as sprayers, sprinklers and feeding attachments.

Secateurs: For pruning stems up to about 1cm diameter. Buy the best general purpose ones you can afford as cheap ones blunt very quickly. However it is always better to buy a good quality 'anvil' pair than a cheap 'scissor' type. You can buy replacement blades for some models. If you have a weak grip choose ones with a ratchet mechanism.

Garden shears: For hedge trimming, but they are hard work. Buy a good pair and keep them sharp but invest in an electric hedge trimmer instead if you have more than a small amount of hedging.

Pruning saw: For larger branches, about the thickness of a broom handle or larger.

Dibber: Cheap and invaluable for planting bulbs, seeds and seedlings.

Sieve: For removing stones and lumps from soil and compost. You may not need one, especially to begin with.

Edging tools: You may find half-moon cutters and long-handled shears useful for keeping your lawn looking smart. An electric trimmer is a labour-saving alternative if you are not a perfectionist.

Lawn mower: Buy the right size and power for the amount of grass you have and the complexity of your lawn's shape. Take time to choose and buy from a helpful, knowledgeable dealer. You will need to mow once a week throughout the summer while your lawn is growing so make sure you buy a machine that you are happy with. Also consider the effect you want – do you want a bowling-green,

a country meadow or something in between? Is your lawn bumpy, flat or sloping? Most mowers nowadays are electric, but a petrol-driven model will be necessary if there isn't a socket handy. Choose from cylinder mowers, rotary mowers and hover mowers and buy a good make with a service centre nearby. Hand mowers are only for tiny lawns or the very athletic. Mowers with small or no grass boxes create extra work.

Garden gloves and kneelers: For comfort and protection of your hands and knees. Fabric gloves with suede patches are best. Some kneelers have tall handles and convert into a seat, an old cushion may do just as well.

plants for sun and shade

MOST PLANTS WILL NATURALLY THRIVE in a sunny or semi-shaded position. Of course not all of your garden will be blessed with sun throughout the day and some parts of it may even be in continual shadow. It is important to know where plants are happiest growing.

Shade-loving plants are more likely to be foliage plants but their lack of flowers does not stop them from creating an interesting effect.

Plants for Sun

Abutilon
Agapanthus
Artemisia
Azalea
Brassica (ornamental cabbage)
Buddleia (butterfly bush)
Campanula
Cistus
Clematis
Dianthus
Echinops (globe thistle)
Fuchsia
Gypsophila
Hebe
Ipomoea (morning glory)
Lavandula (lavender)
Lilium (lily)
Nigella (love-in-a-mist)
Paeonia (peony)
Passiflora (passion flower)
Petunia
Philadelphus (mock orange)
Rosa (rose)
Rosmarinus (rosemary)
Salvia (sage)
Sempervivum (houseleek)
Syringa (lilac)
Tropaeolum (nasturtium)
Tulipa (tulip)
Vitis (grape vine)
Wisteria

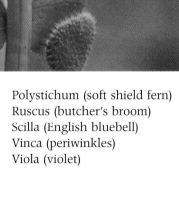

Plants for Shade

Anemone (windflower)
Asplenium (hart's tongue fern)
Berberidopsis
Buxus (box)
Camellia
Convallaria (lily-of-the-valley)
Cotoneaster
Cyclamen
Euonymus

Fatshedera
Forsythia
Fritillaria (snake's head fritil-lary)
Helleborus (Lenten rose)
Hosta (plantain lily)
Hydrangea
Ilex (holly)
Impatiens
Jasminum (jasmine)

Kerria (batchelor's buttons)
Lunaria (honesty)
Mahonia
Meconopsis (Himalayan blue poppy)
Muscari (grape hyacinth)
Myosotis (forget-me-not)
Nicotiana (tobacco plant)
Parthenocissus (virgina creeper)

Polystichum (soft shield fern)
Ruscus (butcher's broom)
Scilla (English bluebell)
Vinca (periwinkles)
Viola (violet)

tasks

ONE OF THE GREAT PLEASURES OF GARDENING is the constant effect of the changing seasons. There is always plenty to do and planning your workload month-by-month is a good way to make sure everything gets done – and at the best time. As local conditions can vary, ask at the nursery where you buy your plants for advice on recommended planting and pruning times.

January

Plant trees, shrubs and perennials. Clean and oil tools. Get your lawnmower serviced.

Look through seed catalogues and send off your orders. Make a new compost heap.

Spread manure on rose beds. Prune wisteria and vines. Wrap terracotta and stone pots and ornaments in hessian or old sheets in very icy weather. Treat or paint exposed ironwork or woodwork.

February

Plant roses. Build a rockery. Start sowing seeds in the greenhouse: lobelia, impatiens, nicotiana, begonias, African marigolds and stocks. Prune late-flowering clematis and winter-flowering shrubs as the flowers fade. Take stem cuttings of chrysanthemums.

March

Ventilate your greenhouse on sunny days and shade seedlings. Prune buddleia, bush and climbing roses, hydrangeas and hardy fuchsias. Prune shrubs grown for their colourful winter stems, such as dogwood, to just above the ground. Hoe beds. Lift and divide hardy perennials and rearrange borders. Feed roses and border plants then mulch soil with bark chippings when the soil is moist. Rake dead leaves off the lawn, as long as it isn't too wet, and spike to aerate. Start mowing with the blade on its highest setting, waiting until any bulb foliage has died down. Plant strawberries, lily bulbs, winter jasmine, mahonia and hardy annuals outdoors. Remove protection from tender plants to prevent early sprouting.

April

Plant out gladioli. If you have a greenhouse, plant hanging baskets and keep them inside until after the last frost. Plant alpines and rock plants. Weed rockeries and fill gaps. Sow herbs.

Plant out sweet pea seedlings. Trim lavender and winter heathers. Sprinkle your lawn with spring fertiliser, trim edgings and resow or turf any bald patches. Start mowing once a week. Sow or turf new lawns. Give tall border plants sticks to grow up, tied loosely to allow for growth. Lay any new paving, repair retaining walls. Train climbers by regularly tying new growth to supports with soft twine.

May

Harden off bedding plants. Mow grass at least once a week on low setting. Prune clematis and forsythia just as they finish flowering and trim rock plants after they flower. Spread a layer of bark chips over moist soil in beds to prevent weeds and conserve moisture. Hoe regularly.

If you don't have a greenhouse, plant hanging baskets and window boxes now. Plant asters and French marigolds directly in the soil for flowering later this year. Sow biennials such as Sweet William, wallflowers, forget-me-nots, polyanthus and foxglove in beds or boxes for flowering next year. Plant dahlia tubers. Trim box topiary. May is a good month to make a pond.

June

June can be very dry so regularly water (and feed) shrubs and trees planted since last winter.

Your greenhouse may start to get very hot so open vents in the day – remembering to close them at night – and paint the glass with a shading wash. Dampen the floor to keep the atmosphere humid. Plant out summer bedding plants as the danger of frost is now over. Water and feed container plants regularly. Check that the ties on staked trees and plants are not too tight and that there is room for growth. Regularly secure new growth of climbers. Cut back herbs and nip off buds for bushiness and extra flavour. Cut aubrieta back to about 8cm to get a good show next year. Prune vines. Give privet and other fast-growing hedges their first clip, tapering in towards the top to allow light to reach all the way down. Spray roses regularly with pesticide and remove suckers.

July

Water hanging baskets every day and feed weekly. Deadhead sweet peas to keep blooms coming and give weekly liquid feed. Trim evergreen shrubs and clip hedges. Deadhead hybrid tea and floribunda roses to keep them flowering then spray for greenfly. Dig some rose fertiliser around the roots. Tie-in and train new growth on climbing plants. Give wisteria its summer pruning. Prune straw-berries and remove the straw or other material that you laid to protect the berries, then fertilise and water well. Slugs may attack hostas and lilies around this time so you may need to take precautionary measures.

August

Feed and water borders regularly. Water hanging baskets and containers daily. Take pelargonium cuttings. Cut herbs such as mint, chives and marjoram back to between 8 and 15 cm high to encourage fresh winter growth. Feed and water dahlias and chrysanthemums regularly and de-bud for extra large blooms. Using a fork or rake, clear any algae from your pond. Leave it in a pile by the bank for a few days to allow any creatures to find their way back into the water. Plant autumn flowering crocuses and cyclamen. Plant strawberries for next year. Clip hedges and prune rambling roses after flowering.

September

Dig up gladioli, chrysanthemums and dahlias before signs of frost. Sow or turf new lawns.
Plant evergreens now or in October. Plant

bulbs for the spring over the next few weeks, except tulips that wait until November. Clean out and disinfect the greenhouse and wash off any exterior shading. Put wire netting across ponds to keep dead leaves out. Clear leaves off rockeries. Order trees and shrubs for autumn planting.

October

Clear away summer annuals from containers and beds. Trim box topiary. Protect the roots of tender plants such as fuchsia or passion flower from frost with a thick circle of straw or bark, about 40 cm across. Remove leaves from ponds. Sweep leaves from the rest of the garden and add them to the compost heap or stack separately to form leaf mould. Weed the garden thoroughly and dispose of all decaying plant material to avoid pests. Rake and spike lawn and apply dressing if it's looking patchy. Re-sow or turf bald spots. Dig over the soil in beds and add manure or compost. Plant spring bedding plants such as wallflowers, forget-me-nots and polyanthus then water well. Take

hardwood cuttings from deciduous shrubs such as forsythia, laurel, privet, shrub roses and buddleia. Slugs and snails are very active at this time of year.

November

Complete planting of tulip and other spring-flowering bulbs. Start planting bare-root trees and shrubs for best root establishment. Cut the lawn for the last time and put cleaned mower away. Make new lawns from turf. Sweep fallen leaves. Cut down border perennials. Clean out greenhouse and wash down if you haven't done this already.

December

Check that recently planted trees and shrubs are securely staked to cope with winter winds and that ties haven't come loose. Continue planting evergreens, trees, roses and shrubs. Dig up and replant border perennials. Plant large-flowered clematis. Knock heavy snow from evergreen branches to prevent them snapping off.
Send off for seed catalogues.

index

Picture Credits

Special photography by Polly Wreford, styling by Claudia Bryant. Mosaic table designed and made by Tessa Brown.
Arcaid /M Ashby 63 /A Held 30 /G Lung /Belle 47; **Camera Press** /Avotakka 28; **Garden Picture Library** /B Thomas 27 /D Askham 0 (Hampton Court Flower Show) /F Strauss 18, 34, 42-43, 80 /G Roger 7 Centre Right, 10 /H Rice 56 (HCtFS 1997), 64 /J S Sira 70,86 /J Hurst 66 /J Legate 50, 53 /J Sorrell 76 /J Ferro Sims 60, 66 /J Glover 2 Centre 29, 68, 81, 82 (HCtFS 1995 Designer C Costin), 88 (CFS National Asthma Campaign) /J Miller 12 /J Bouchier 28 /J Wade Back cover, 59 (Old Chapel, Glos. NGS), 90 /Lamontagne 34 /L Burgess 17 /L Brotchie 4, 23, 18,19, 33, 74, 83, 84 /M O'Hara 16, 22, 35, 52 /Mayer /le Scanff 73 (Jardin de Campagne), 85 (Jardin de Anne Marie), 94, 95 /N Francis 23 /N Temple 13 /R Evans 69 /R Sutherland 24 (CFS 1997, Designer F Lawrenson /BSB), 26, 27 (CFS 1994 Designer D Pearson /Evening Standard), 42, 50 (CFS 1997 Designer S Shire), 62 Right (Designer A Paul), 62 left (CFS 1994 Designer C Bradley-Hole), 78 (Designer P Flinton), 79, 82 Top right (CFS 1994 Designer J Adams), 86 left (Designer A Paul) /S Wooster 17, 30 (L Morrow), 32, 75, 76 (Designers C Boardman & S Blackie) /S Harte 38; **John Glover** /5 Top Right, 8, 56, 68 (CFS 1994 P Tinsley), 88. **Octopus Publishing Group Ltd.** /A Lawson 92 /J Harpur 92, 93 /M Boys 92, 93 /S Wooster 12, 73, 77. **Robert Harding Picture Library** /A Von Einsiedel 39 (Homes & Gardens, R Harding Syndication) /D Patterson Endpapers, Front lap (Homes & Gardens, R.Harding syndication), 91 (Homes & Gardens, R Harding Syndication) /N McDiarmid 6 Top Left, 44, 45 (Homes & Gardens, R Harding Syndication). **Jerry Harpur** /51 (Designer J Fearnley-whittingstall), 72, 74, 84 (Designer D Ross). **Clive Nichols Photography** /82 (CFS 1994 Designer P Hobhouse), 58 (Designers R & J Passmore), 60 (CFS 1994/Home Farm Trust), 32 (Keukenhof, Holland), 89 (CFS 1993 /Monk Sherbourne), 67 (CFS 1996/Pro Carton Garden), 87 (CFS 1993/Woking Borough Council). **Photos Horticultural** /38, 44, 52; **Elizabeth Whiting & Associates** /D Lewis 46 (Top), 46 J Tubby.

First published in the U.K. in 1998 by Hamlyn an imprint of Octopus Publishing Group Limited 2–4 Heron Quays London E14 4JP

Copyright © 1998 Octopus Publishing Group Limited

Distributed in the United States and Canada by Sterling Publishing Co., Inc. 387 Park Avenue South New York, NY 10016–8810

This paperback edition copyright © 2000 Octopus Publishing Group Limited

All rights reserved. No part of this publication may be reproduced, stored in a retrieval system, or transmitted, in any form or by any means, electronic, electrostatic, magnetic tape, mechanical, photocopying, recording or otherwise without the prior permission in writing of the publisher.

ISBN 0 600 60102 1

Produced by Toppan

Printed in China